Brian Thompson

PUFFIN
FIRST
PICTURE
DICTIONARY

Illustrated by Celia Berridge

PUFFIN BOOKS
———————
VIKING KESTREL

Brian Thompson is a primary school head teacher in Richmond upon Thames, Surrey. He is well known for his work on Longman's highly successful Breakthrough to Literacy scheme and has compiled several story and poetry collections for children. Born and brought up in Australia, he has lived in Britain for many years.

Celia Berridge is a well-known children's books illustrator, most notably of the *Postman Pat* books, but also *Forget-Me-Not* and *Sheepchase* by Paul Rogers. She has done considerable research, both at Brighton Polytechnic and at Sussex University, into children's perception of pictures. As well as illustrating, she is a part-time tutor in the post-graduate graphic design course at the Central School of Art in London.

PUFFIN BOOKS/VIKING KESTREL

Published by the Penguin Group
27 Wrights Lane, London W8 5TZ, England
Viking Penguin Inc., 40 West 23rd Street, New York, New York 10010, USA
Penguin Books Australia Ltd, Ringwood, Victoria, Australia
Penguin Books Canada Ltd, 2801 John Street, Markham, Ontario, Canada L3R 1B4
Penguin Books (NZ) Ltd, 182-190 Wairau Road, Auckland 10, New Zealand

Penguin Books Ltd, Registered Offices: Harmondsworth, Middlesex, England

First published in Great Britain by Puffin/Viking Kestrel 1988
and simultaneously in the USA by Viking Kestrel
3 5 7 9 10 8 6 4 2

Filmset in Century Schoolbook (Linotron 202) by
Rowland Phototypesetting Ltd, 30 Oval Road, London NW1 7DE
Printed and bound in Great Britain by
William Clowes Limited, Beccles and London

British Library Cataloguing in Publication Data
Thompson, Brian, 1938 –
Puffin first picture dictionary
(Picture Puffin).
1. Vocabulary – Pictorial works –
Juvenile literature
I. Title II. Berridge, Celia
428.1'022'2   PE1449

ISBN Paperback 0 14 050.777 9
ISBN Hardback 0-670-81802-X

Aa

apple

ant

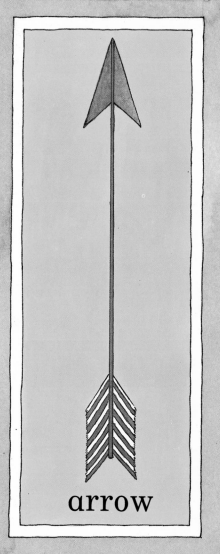

arrow

astronaut

avocado

Bb

ball

balloon

basket

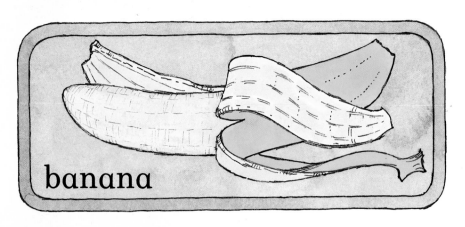

banana

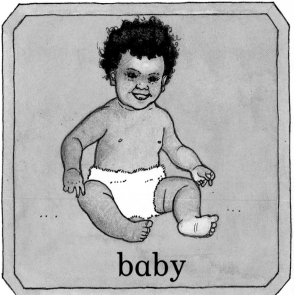

baby

Bb

black

bear

bicycle

bird

Bb

blue

book

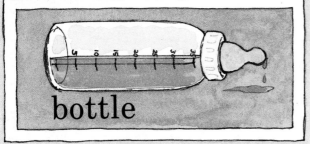

bottle

boat

bridge

Bb

brown

button

bricks

butterfly

Cc

car

cat

camel

caterpillar

camera

Cc

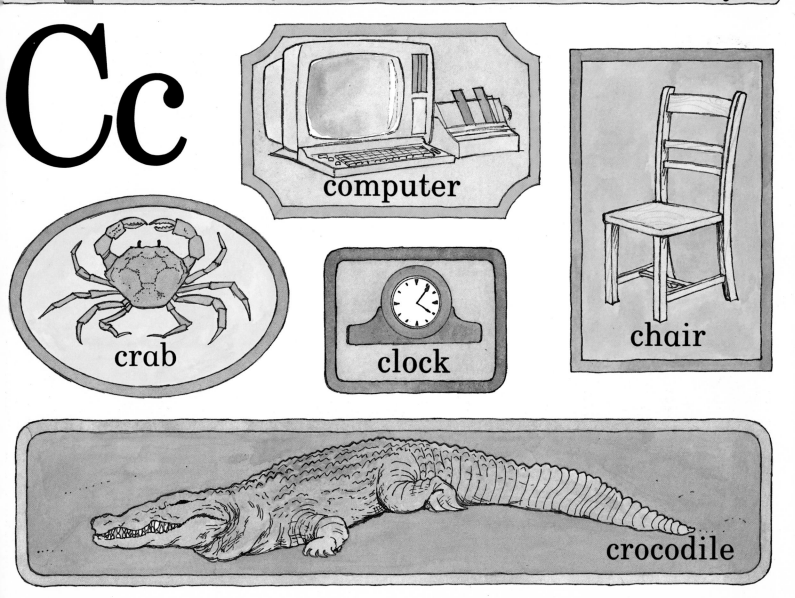

computer

crab

clock

chair

crocodile

Dd

doll

dog

door

dinosaur

Dd

dragon

dress

drum

duck

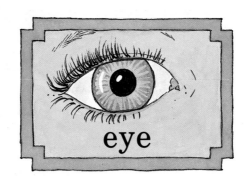

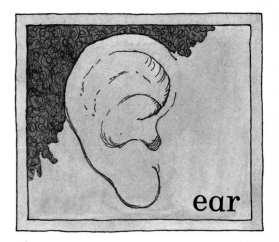

Ee

eye

egg

elephant

ear

Ff

five

fence

fish

fire

Ff

flag

fly

flower

fork

four

Ff

fruit

fountain

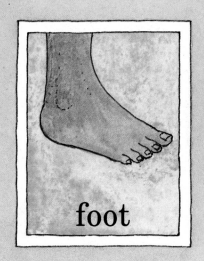

foot

frog

Gg

gate

giraffe

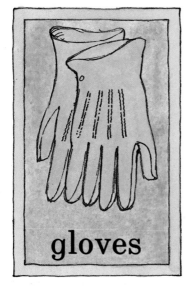

gloves

giant

Gg

goat

goldfish

grapes

green

guitar

Hh

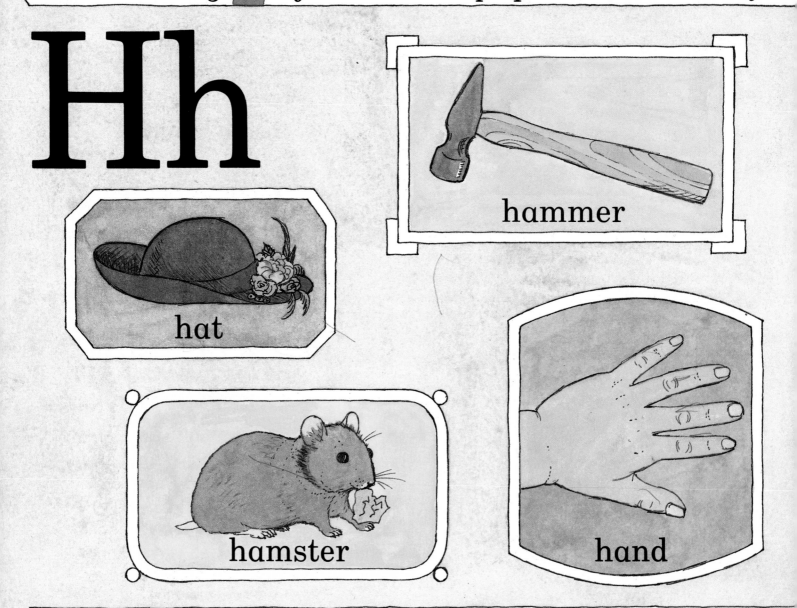

hammer

hat

hamster

hand

Hh

house

hen

helicopter

horse

Ii

ice

iceberg

ink

ice-cream

island

Jj

jug

juggler

jacket

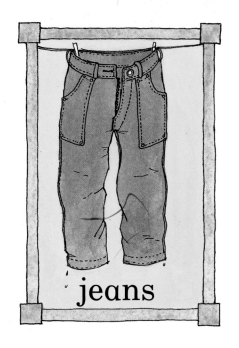

jeans

jigsaw

Kk

kettle

kangaroo

knife

knitting

key

Ll

log

lemon

ladder

lion

leaf

Mm

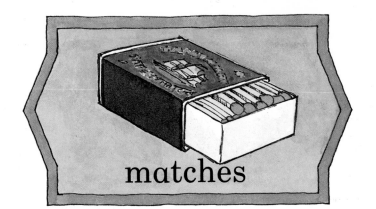
matches

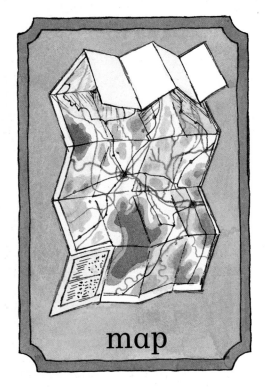
map

magnet

milk

a b c d e f g h i j k l **m** n o p q r s t u v w x y z

Mm

moon

monkey

motorcycle

mouse

A B C D E F G H I J K L **M** N O P Q R S T U V W X Y Z

Nn

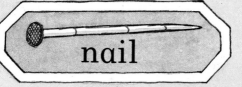

nail

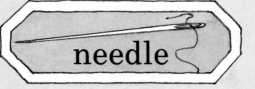

needle

nuts

net

nurses

nest

Oo

one

1

orange

octopus

owl

ostrich

oranges

P p

panda

parrot

paints

parachute

Pp

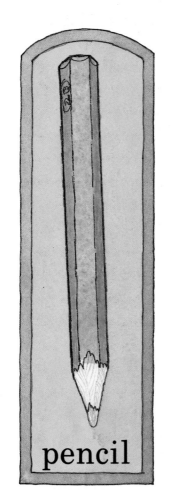

pencil

penguin

pink

pig

Pp

pin

pigeon

piano

puppy

Qq

quail

quilt

queen

Rr

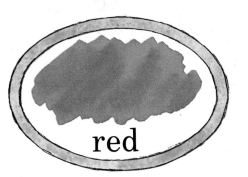

red

radio

rainbow

rabbit

Rr

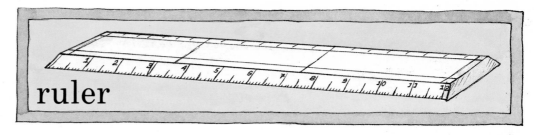

ruler

ring

robot

rope

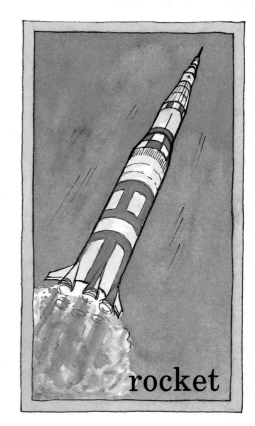

rocket

Ss

saw

scissors

sheep

sand castle

shark

Ss

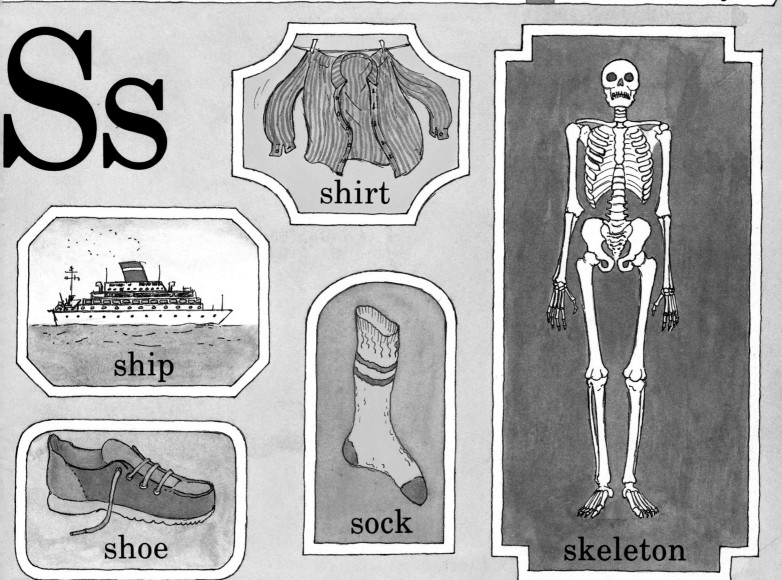

shirt

ship

shoe

sock

skeleton

Ss

spider

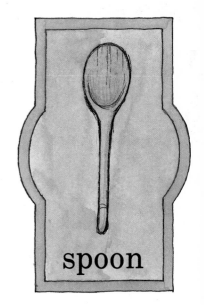
spoon

snowman

snake

snail

Ss

stamp

submarine

swing

star

string

Tt

table

television

telephone

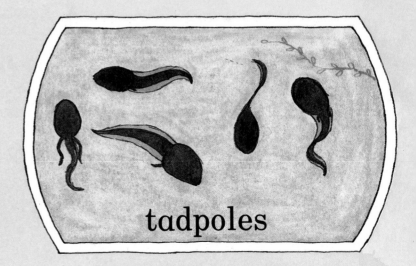

tadpoles

Tt

three

tiger

tent

teddy bear

Tt

tortoise

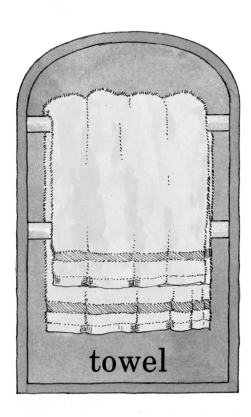

towel

tomato

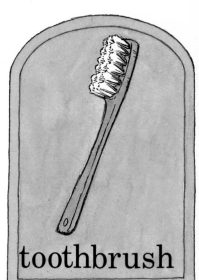

toothbrush

Tt

train

tree

tractor

trumpet

2

two

Uu

underwear

umbrella

unicorn